The Legend Of The North Star

(Little Dot Makes A Wish)

A Christmas Story
And A Play For Children

Donna J. Fetzer

CSS Publishing Company, Inc., Lima, Ohio

THE LEGEND OF THE NORTH STAR
(Little Dot Makes A Wish)

Copyright © 2007 by
CSS Publishing Company, Inc.
Lima, Ohio

For more information about CSS Publishing Company resources, visit our website at www.csspub.com or email us at csr@csspub.com or call (800) 241-4056.

Cover design by Barbara Spencer

ISBN: 978-0-7880-2570-9

PRINTED IN USA

*I dedicate this story and play
to all my grandchildren and stepgrandchildren.
They are the reason I write.*

Introduction

This story is written in two forms. The first is a story to be read or told to Sunday school classes or at church events such as banquets or Christmas programs.

The second form is a play that is perfect for Christmas. All ages can participate in the production for an outreach event.

The Legend Of
The North Star
(Little Dot Makes A Wish)

A Christmas Story

The Legend Of The North Star
(Little Dot Makes A Wish)

In the beginning God created day and night, light and
darkness, and created the stars that shine like diamonds.

Many, many years ago, stars were placed in the dark skies to
light up the night. One, lone, tiny black dot was left behind. The
lonely little dot rolled and darted here and there, around thousands
and thousands of glowing points of light.

The little dot heard the names of Orion, Sirius, and Aquarius,
but he never heard his name. "What's my name?" he asked all the
bigger stars. Many of the stars winked and blinked and slipped
away.

One day, stars in the galaxy called the Milky Way gave the tiny
dot a name. They called him Little Dot. "Thank you, thank you,"
he said. Then he asked the stars, "Why don't I glow ... Why am I
not big and bright? I just want to be as shiny as the other stars."

One of the largest stars in the Milky Way said, "Don't worry,
Little Dot. One day you will be big and you will shine brightly."

"Today would be a good day," Little Dot said. "I could shine
and glow and be seen by everyone. Oh, how I wish I could be like
the other stars."

Luminaria, wisest of all stars, heard Little Dot. She glided close
to him. "I'm giving you one wish," she said. "You must use it wisely,
and only when you really need it ... not before," she warned. "Do
you think you can do that?"

Little Dot was so excited he did a double roll. "Yes, I can do
that!" he answered. "But I already know what my wish is ... I'd like
to be the most brilliant star ever."

Sounds of Luminaria's laughter filled the night stars. Glitter
flew all about. "That's a very good dream, Little Dot," she said.
"But you must remember not to use your wish foolishly." Then in a
twinkling of a star, she was gone.

Little Dot thought and thought. "How will I use my wish? Maybe I could become a *rock and roll star.* That would be awesome." He began to play an air guitar, rocking to music only he could hear. "Nooo, that might be considered foolish." He rolled around in the sky thinking, "I know. I could blink on and off at will, fooling all the people below." That made him chuckle. "Wait, I've got it ... I could wish to be a comet with a long, trailing tail of light. That would be beautiful." Little Dot closed his eyes, dreaming. "Maybe I could be a meteor — a shooting star. People on earth believe that if you see a shooting star and make a wish, it will come true." He opened his eyes. "That won't work. How would I get back up in the sky if I fell to Earth? Oh, thinking is such hard work."

Then one night when Little Dot was busy thinking and thinking, he heard the tinkling voices of all the stars. Something was happening down on Earth. Little Dot flew through the clouds, searching for Luminaria. "What's going on?" he asked. "Everyone sounds so excited, and I don't know what's happening."

"Let me tell you," Luminaria whispered. "Look closely, and listen carefully. Can you see the fields outside the town of Bethlehem?"

Little Dot peeked through the clouds. "Yes, I do."

"Can you see the shepherds watching over their flocks of sheep?"

"Yes, yes! I do."

"Do you see how light the dark sky is becoming?"

"It is lighter! I see the shepherds looking up in the sky!" he said. "Can they see me?"

"No, Little Dot, they can't see you, but they can see the angel."

"I see the angel, too!" he shouted. "The shepherds look afraid. What's the matter?"

"Shhhhh, listen, Little Dot," Luminaria said, "the angel is speaking."

I am bringing you news of great joy. Tonight in the city of Bethlehem, a Savior has been born. He is called Jesus Christ and he is our Lord.

10

Luminaria whispered in Little Dot's ear. "That's why all the stars are excited. The angel is looking for a special star to lead three wise men from the Far East, who have been watching the night skies for many years. They believe that some day a new star will rise to announce the birth of their king."

Little Dot nearly rolled out of the sky. "A new star! I could be that star! I wish to be the brightest, the most brilliant and shiny star in the sky." Luminaria glistened brightly and nodded.

Three wise men were riding on their camels bearing gifts for the Christ Child. They saw the brightest star they had ever seen in the night sky. They followed the light of that brilliant star to Bethlehem. The star stopped above the stable where Jesus lay in a manger — fulfilling God's plan. The three wise men raised their gifts high over their heads in thanks.

Little Dot got his wish. He *was* that shining star, and he was given his true name — the Star of Bethlehem.

The End

The Legend Of
The North Star
(Little Dot Makes A Wish)

A Christmas Play
For Youth Of All Ages

The Legend Of The North Star
(Little Dot Makes A Wish)

Summary

A storyteller tells the "Legend Of The North Star," a story about Little Dot, who was left behind in the night sky after all the stars had been created. Little Dot is curious as to why he doesn't have a name, and why he doesn't look like the other stars in the sky. Luminaria, the wisest of all stars, heard Little Dot make a wish to be like the other stars. She grants him one wish. After Little Dot thinks of several humorous ways to use his wish, Luminaria returns and helps him discover his real name and his purpose. He becomes the Star of Bethlehem.

Characters

Storyteller

Luminaria — wisest of all stars, gives Little Dot a wish he must use wisely

Little Dot — left behind after God created the stars

Orion, Sirius, Aquarius — stars

Milky Way — a galaxy of stars (several children can be the galaxy)

Angel

Joseph (nonspeaking)

Mary (nonspeaking)

Three Wise Men (nonspeaking)

Shepherds — two or three (nonspeaking)

Little Stars and Clouds (nonspeaking)

Choir — adult and/or junior (nonspeaking)

Props

Two high stools draped with white netting and tinsel (to look like clouds)

One low stool (decorated as above)

15

Chair (decorated as above)
Two or three low palm trees
Cardboard sheep
Shepherds' staffs with cardboard sheep attached
Staff
Baby Jesus (doll wrapped in white cloth)
Manger
Lightweight silver pole with brilliant star attached
Battery-operated blinking Christmas lights (one for each star)
Gifts
Large book
Pouches to hold tinsel
Tiny bells
Pen lights, battery-operated candles, or flashlights (optional)

Costumes

Storyteller — white flowing robe, a shiny headdress, ballerina slippers

Little Stars — white robes with tinsel streamers, blinking star headdresses, white ballerina slippers

Choir — white, flowing robes, blinking star headdresses, white ballerina slippers, pouches of Christmas tinsel

Joseph and Shepherds — robes, head scarves, staffs, sandals

Mary — long, blue dress, head scarf, shawl, sandals, carrying doll

Little Dot — all in black — black slippers (no flip-flops or sandals); later all in silver

Luminaria — silvery, flowing gown with lots of tinsel attached, bright blinking star headdress, white ballerina slippers, pouch of tinsel

Clouds — white netting and tinsel made into fluffy clouds, white tights, fluffy headdress, white ballerina slippers, pouches of tinsel

Angel — long, flowing dress, wings, halo with tinsel streamers, white ballerina slippers

Setting
   The play takes place in the sky before Christmas Eve. The lights are low. The backdrop is painted dark with twinkling stars (blinking Christmas lights) and white clouds made from white netting and Christmas tinsel. The stage should have three levels: a platform, risers, and lower stage area. The choir will be on the risers, each dressed in white with a star headdress. There will be actors dressed as stars and clouds on the platform in the background. The set should give the illusion of being in the sky.
   On the platform is one cloud chair stage right, two high cloud stools, and one low cloud stool stage left. On the lower level of stage left are two or three low palm trees and sheep. Storyteller has a large book she reads from. Offstage right is a manger to be brought center stage as the choir sings. Mary and Joseph enter at that time.

(It is night. The stars are twinkling. Children dressed as stars and clouds are in the background. The choir is standing on the risers. Storyteller enters stage right carrying a large book. She sits on the cloud chair, opens the book, and motions for Little Stars to come.)

Storyteller: Come, my twinkling little stars and I will tell you about the legend of the North Star. *(Little Stars gather around the Storyteller to hear the legend)* In the beginning God created day and night, light and darkness, and created the stars that shine like diamonds. Many years ago, stars were placed in the dark skies to light up the night. One lone, tiny black dot was left behind after the stars were placed in the sky. The lonely little dot rolled and darted here and there, around thousands and thousands of glowing points of light.

(Little Stars stand, face the audience, put their arms around each other, rocking back and forth as they sing, "Twinkle, Twinkle, Little Star." Little Dot, doing a cartwheel enters stage left and stops center stage. Orion, Sirius, Aquarius enter stage right from the background scene and float around Little Dot.)

17

Orion, Sirius, Aquarius: *(playfully)* Hi, I'm Orion. This is Sirius and Aquarius. We're important stars. Who ... are you?

Little Dot: *(looks unhappy)* I'm, I'm ... I don't know. I'm just a dot in the night sky. I don't have a name.

Orion, Sirius, Aquarius: That's too bad ... maybe some day ...

(Waving, Orion, Sirius, and Aquarius join the stars in the background. Little Dot floats over to other stars.)

Storyteller: The little dot wanted a name. He asked all the bigger stars if they knew his name. They just blinked and winked and slipped away. The stars didn't have an answer.

(Milky Way, a galaxy of several stars, enters together from the background scene.)

Storyteller: One day, a galaxy called the Milky Way, floated beside the little dot.

(Milky Way floats to Little Dot.)

Milky Way: *(only one star speaks)* I know you would like a name. We heard it from the star-line, and we have just the perfect name for you. *(Other Milky Way stars nod and agree)* Yes, yes, the perfect name.

Little Dot: *(uncertain)* Really?

Milky Way: You will be called Little Dot.

Little Dot: *(excitedly)* Thank you, thank you. I love my name. *(downcast)* But ... why don't I glow like the other stars? Why am I not big and bright? I just want to be as shiny as the other stars.

Milky Way: *(only one star speaks)* Don't worry, Little Dot. One day you will be big, and you will shine brightly. *(all start to leave)*

Little Dot: *(enthusiastically)* Wait ... today would be a good day. I could shine and glow and be seen by everyone.

(Milky Way stars giggle, tiny bells ring as they exit.)

Little Dot: *(sighs)* Oh, how I wish I could be like the other stars. *(sits down on the cloud stool)*

Storyteller: Luminaria, wisest of all stars, heard Little Dot make that wish.

(Luminaria enters stage right. She floats close to Little Dot.)

Luminaria: Hello, Little Dot. I am Luminaria, the wisest of all stars. I heard you make a wish.

Little Dot: *(surprised, jumps up)* Luminaria!

Luminaria: *(smiles)* Yes, and I am going to grant you one wish ... only one. You must use it wisely, and only when you really need it ... and not before. Do you think you can do that?

Little Dot: *(excitedly)* Yes, yes, I can do that! But I already know what my wish is ... I'd like to be the most brilliant star ever.

Luminaria: *(motherly)* That's a very good dream, Little Dot. But you must remember not to use your wish foolishly.

(Tiny bells ring and tinsel falls from above as Luminaria exits.)

Storyteller: Well, Little Dot was very excited. He began thinking and thinking how he might use that one and only wish.

Little Dot: *(thinking, he strolls back and forth)* How will I use my wish? *(stops walking)*

Maybe ... I could become a rock and roll star. Yesss! *(begins playing an air guitar and dancing to music only he can hear, then stops playing)* Nooo, that might be considered foolish. *(sits down, thinks, jumps up)*

I know, I could blink on and off at will, fooling all the people below. *(chuckles)*

Wait, I've got it ... I could wish to be a, uh, comet, with a long trailing tail of light *(motions a long tail of light behind him, then nods and sits down)* Yes, yes ... that would be beautiful. *(closes his eyes and dreams)*

Or, maybe a meteor ... a shooting star. People on earth believe that if you see a shooting star and make a wish, it will come true. *(opens his eyes and jumps up)* That won't work. How would I get back up in the sky if I fell to Earth? *(sits down on the cloud stool in the position of The Thinker)* Oh, thinking is such hard work.

Storyteller: Then one night, when Little Dot was busy thinking and thinking, he heard the tinkling voices of all the stars.

(Tiny little bells ring. Little Dot stands up and looks up, down, and all around.)

Storyteller: Something was happening down on Earth. Little Dot flew through clouds, searching for Luminaria.

(Little Dot floats around the Stars and Clouds looking for Luminaria.)

Little Dot: Luminaria, Luminaria, where are you?

(Luminaria enters as the tinkling bells continue to ring softly.)

Luminaria: *(reassuringly)* I'm right here, Little Dot. Come and sit with me.

Little Dot: *(worried)* What's going on? Everyone sounds so excited, and I don't know what's happening.

(Little Dot and Luminaria sit on the two high stools, and look below. Choir sings "O Little Town Of Bethlehem." Shepherds enter from stage left, carrying staffs with sheep attached. One stands, one sits beside the palm trees.)

Luminaria: *(when the Choir stops, whispers)* Let me tell you, Little Dot, what is happening. Look closely, and listen carefully. *(points)* Can you see the fields outside the town of Bethlehem?

Little Dot: Yes, I do.

Luminaria: Can you see the shepherds watching over their flocks of sheep?

Little Dot: Yes, yes, I do!

Luminaria: Do you see how light the dark sky is becoming?

(Lights are slowly turned up.)

Little Dot: *(amazed)* It is lighter! I see the shepherds looking up in the sky! Can they see me?

Luminaria: No, Little Dot, they can't see you, but they can see the angel below.

(Choir sings verse 1 of "While Shepherds Watched Their Flocks By Night." The Angel appears and stands on the risers above the Shepherds. The Shepherds look up and appear to be frightened.)

Little Dot: *(loudly)* I see the angel, too. The shepherds look afraid. What's the matter?

Luminaria: *(whispers)* Shhhh, listen, Little Dot. The angel is speaking.

Angel: I am bringing you news of great joy. Tonight in the city of Bethlehem, a Savior has been born. He is called Jesus Christ and he is our Lord.

(Choir sings verses 2 and 3 of "While Shepherds Watched Their Flocks By Night." The manger is moved to center stage.)

Luminaria: *(whispers)* That's why all the stars are excited. The angel is looking for a special star to lead the three wise men from the Far East, who have been watching the night skies for many years. They believe that some day a new star will rise to announce the birth of their king.

Little Dot: *(stands, does two cartwheels, then sits back down)* Wow! They are looking for a new star.

Luminaria: *(laughs; tiny bells ring)* Yes, that is true.

Little Dot: *(elatedly)* A new star! I could be that star! *(stands, arms outstretched, and looks up)* I wish to be the brightest, the most brilliant and shiny star in the sky.

Luminaria: *(nods and smiles)* Wish granted.

(Luminaria and Little Dot exit. Many tiny bells ring and lots of tinsel falls from above. Little Stars and Clouds sing "Away In The Manger." Mary and Joseph enter stage right. Mary sits beside the manger, holding a baby. Joseph stands beside her. Shepherds carry their staffs with sheep attached, and stand on either side of Mary and Joseph. Little Dot enters stage left on the risers and waits until the singing stops. He is now dressed in silver, carrying a silver pole with a bright, twinkling star attached. Choir sings "We Three Kings." Little Dot walks slowly to center stage and holds the star over the stable scene. Three Wise Men, carrying their gifts, enter

22

from the back and walk slowly down the center aisle as Choir sings. They pause partway and point to the star. They continue to the stage and kneel in front of Mary and Joseph. The singing stops.)

Storyteller: Three wise men were riding on their camels, bearing gifts for the Christ Child. They saw the brightest star they had ever seen in the night sky. They followed the light of that brilliant star to Bethlehem. The star stopped above the stable where Jesus lay in a manger, fulfilling God's plan.

(Choir sings "What Child Is This?")

Storyteller: Little Dot got his wish. He was that shining star ...

(Storyteller and Little Stars stand facing the audience, stretch out their arms and look up.)

Storyteller: He was given his true name ... the Star of Bethlehem.

(With bells ringing and tinsel falling from above, Little Stars hold hands and skip in a circle around Storyteller. They skip left, skip right, and end by kneeling with their hands in prayer position, looking up at Little Dot.)

(Audience and all actors sing "Go Tell It On The Mountain.")

The End